*So You're
Planning a Wedding*

So You're Planning a Wedding

by

C. D. Hansen

Beacon Hill Press of Kansas City
Kansas City, Missouri

First Printing, 1976

ISBN: 0-8341-0418-0

Printed in the
United States of America

10 9

Contents

Preface

This booklet is not written as a comprehensive study of wedding etiquette. Rather, its purpose is to put in capsule form some necessary and established protocol and to provide a brief planning guide for couples to use in planning their weddings. There are many contemporary ideas that can be worked into the ceremony by the bride and groom that will make their wedding unique. Therefore, the reader should consider this book as only a basic guide incorporating some rules that should be observed.

If a wedding is to run smoothly, it must be well planned by both bride and groom, with consideration being given to the wishes of the parents of each. The minister who is to officiate must also be consulted; for, after all, the ceremony is a worship service, and it is his right to have a voice in what transpires at the altars of his church.

As you plan and prepare, may these be happy days of anticipation for your "finest hour."

As you step across the threshold into a new and exciting life together, may the Lord be with you.

For parts of this booklet I wish to acknowledge with appreciation the permission granted by Hawthorn Books, Inc., of New York to use material from *The Bride's School: Complete Book of Engagement and Wedding Etiquette,* by Barbara Wilson (1959).

—C. D. Hansen

1

Planning Your Wedding

Marriage is one of life's most significant events and involves the total investment of the lives of the two people who are so joined. It is an "honorable estate" and as such is "not to be entered into unadvisedly, but reverently, discreetly, and in the fear of God."

While marriage is contractual in nature, it must be founded upon more than mere legal bindings or a signed piece of paper. It should be entered into as a lifetime adventure and, above all, should be built upon sound biblical principles. For the Christian, marriage should be more than an ordinary social institution, for it is, "above everything else, 'a holy estate.' Man and wife are no longer twain, but one flesh."

Contrary to popular opinion, marriage is more than a 50-50 proposition; for if the marital relationship is to survive, it must receive 100 percent cooperation from each partner.

Couples being married in either a civil or religious ceremony will take vows to love, to cherish, and to have and to hold regardless of physical circumstances, until they are parted by death.

These vows should not be repeated or treated with an air of flippancy, for they are sacred and holy. It should be pointed out that it is not man, nor state, but God that joins a man and a woman together in "holy wedlock," and those "whom God has joined together, let not man put asunder."

When entered into upon this basis, with plans to make God the Head of your home, your marriage can be both satisfying and lasting.

Basic Decisions

Every wedding must start with plans. Whether the plans are arranged by the bride and her family, the bride and the groom, or with a bridal consultant, the bride must decide what she wants.

Kinds of Weddings

There are at least four types of possible weddings, with many variations to each type:

1. An informal home wedding, usually followed by a small reception in the home, or no reception at all.

2. An informal wedding in the home, with a reception at another public building.

3. A garden wedding, with reception on the lawn or elsewhere in the event of rain.

4. A formal or semiformal ceremony in the church, followed by a reception at the church or at a public building. Naturally there are varying degrees of formality.

Date and Hour

The date and hour of the wedding is a matter of personal choice—within the boundaries, of course, of the rules of the church or the judgment of the officiating clergyman. Therefore, before you finalize any specific time, make an appointment with the clergyman to see if he and the church are available then. If the time is confirmed, you are free to proceed with more detailed plans.

See that specific reservations are made for the church and other facilities, such as the fellowship hall. This should be in writing.

Pastoral Counsel

Most ministers will wish to discuss with you the spiritual aspects of marriage and the sacredness of the vows you are taking. This is an important part of their ministry, and they do this because of their interest in people, especially young couples beginning a new adventure in life such as marriage. It is important to the minister that you understand the implications of marriage, including the possible rearing of children. In all probability he will ask you some pointed questions, not to embarrass you but to help you.

If you are divorced, do not be embarrassed if the minister asks you if you have biblical grounds for your divorce. Many churches, including the Church of the Nazarene, believe that the only such grounds are adultery on the part of your former spouse, with you being the innocent party. If you do not have biblical grounds, he is forbidden by church policy to perform the ceremony (see *Manual,* par. 34.1).

Should your divorce be scriptural and the minister consents to perform the ceremony, there are some basic rules of etiquette that must be followed. For example, usually a divorced person will have a quiet wedding and will not go through an elaborate ceremony. A divorcee does not wear white or a veil, and the giving away of the bride is eliminated.

The Visiting Minister

The wedding will probably be held in the bride's church or that of her parents. This being the case, it is proper for her own minister to perform the service. However, there are exceptions to this procedure.

Perhaps there is a member of either family who is a minister, and you may wish for him to either perform the ceremony or to assist your minister. Should this be the case, you must discuss this matter with your minister, and he will give you advice as to the correct procedure.

Should the bride not have a regular minister, then it is proper for the groom's minister to perform the ceremony.

The Minister's Fee

The payment for the minister's services is to be considered a donation inasmuch as a minister is not usually paid a set fee. The amount of the donation is left to the discretion of the groom and should not be discussed with the minister.

If the fee is paid by check, it should be made out to the minister and not the church. Usually the best man will hand the fee to the minister either in his office or in the foyer of the church. Do not hand it to him in the sanctuary. It should be placed in a white envelope with a thank-you note.

Church Regulations

Every church has certain regulations pertaining to events other than regular church activities or services. Therefore, even if you are a member of the congregation, before you make any final decisions about decorations, music, and so forth, check with the minister to make sure that what you have in mind will be allowed. There could be limitations that will require you to alter your plans. These regulations are established because of past experience and are there of necessity.

It is a good idea to prepare a list of questions in

advance of consultation with the minister. Most ministers will advise you to call them if you have any questions. It is far wiser to get a clarification ahead of time than to come to rehearsal and find something you have planned is contrary to established rules.

In church weddings there are some basic procedures to follow. The church may even have a written policy which must be adhered to. Here are some suggestions to keep in mind.

1. The church is a sacred place of worship; and at the rehearsal and wedding, there should be an attitude of dignity displayed by those participating and attending. Your wedding is as sacred as any worship service—in fact, that is what it is—and it should be treated accordingly.

2. Decorations of the building in any fashion should be cleared with the minister before proceeding with arrangements.

3. Be cautious about moving church furniture. Churches are not usually arranged for weddings, and therefore some furniture must be moved. However, before this is done, discuss the matter with the minister. When furniture is moved, it should be returned to its original place immediately following the wedding. You should instruct your ushers that this will be part of their task, unless the church has an adequate staff and wishes to do it.

4. While most churches do not make a specific charge to their membership for the use of the building, it is appropriate to give a personal donation for the extra burden placed upon the caretaker. This is usually taken care of by the bride's father and can be given at the time of the rehearsal. Most churches do, however, have set fees for persons outside their membership. If the church has a fellowship hall, there will probably be an additional charge if this is used for the reception.

5. If you are expecting a large wedding, it will probab-

ly be necessary for you to supply someone to help with the parking of cars.

6. The organist and soloist, unless they are friends of the couple, will probably have set fees for their services. If you are in doubt as to what this fee is, be free to ask them. If they are members of the church staff, you may ask the minister or his secretary.

7. If you desire canvas aisle carpet, aisle ribbons, or silk ropes, check with the minister or his secretary to see if these are available from the church. If they are not, and you wish to use them, then you must order from a florist or caterer.

Decorations and Flowers

Flowers are an important part of a beautiful wedding and, as such, careful consideration should be given to the purchase of any floral arrangements. For the proper advice as to arrangement and color scheme, you should have a consultation with your local florist to see what is available. However, as with other matters, before placing an order with your florist, it is essential that you consult the minister, the custodian, or the minister's secretary. Some churches may have restrictions as to where flowers may be placed or decorations used. In any event, it is necessary to reserve the time for installation of any decorations.

Music

There is a wide choice of music that can be used at certain times during the wedding ceremony. For example, while the guests are coming into the sanctuary and finding their seats before the ceremony, there should be appropriate prelude music. You may select your own music for this or allow the organist to do it for you.

During the procession of the bridal party up the aisle,

13

the traditional music would probably be Wagner's "Wedding March" from *Lohengrin* ("Here Comes the Bride"). The recessional music might be Mendelssohn's "Wedding March" from *A Midsummer Night's Dream.*

Included in the ceremony can be such traditional songs as "I Love You Truly" and "Oh, Promise Me," but many appropriate new songs could be used instead. A word of caution should be given here. Some modern songs need to be carefully analyzed as to their appropriateness in a religious service. Here, again, the minister should be consulted. Certainly there is a wide enough range of religious music that can be used. To aid you in your selection, here is a listing of some of these songs.

> "Channels Only"
> "Great Is Thy Faithfulness"
> "O Jesus, I [We] Have Promised"
> "O Master, Let Me [Us] Walk with Thee"
> "O Perfect Love"
> "Saviour, My Heart Is Thine"
> "Take My Life, and Let It Be"
> (Take Our Lives, and Let Them Be)

These songs can be found in most church hymnals.

Here is another group of wedding songs that might be of interest and helpful in selecting your wedding music:

> Leonard Bernstein—"One Hand, One Heart"
> Jennie Prince Black—"The Pledge"
> Carl Bohm—"Calm as the Night"
> Dosia Carlson—"A Wedding Blessing"
> Ernest Charles—"Love Is of God"
> Wilbur Chenoweth—"Love, I Come to You"
> Reginald DeHoven—"Oh, Promise Me"
> Roland Diggle—"A Wedding Prayer"
> Fern Glasgow Dunlap—"Wedding Prayer"

Idabelle Firestone—"If I Could Tell You"
Charles Gounod—"Entreat Me Not to Leave Thee"
Edvard Grieg—"I Love Thee"
David Guion—"As We, O Lord, Have Joined Our Hands"
F. Flaxington Harker—"O Perfect Love"
Rena Lesser—"God Bless This Day"
Austin C. Lovelace—"A Wedding Benediction"
Clarence Olmstead—"So Is My Beloved"

Photographs

You will no doubt want pictures of your wedding taken by either an amateur camera bug or a professional photographer. Whoever is responsible for taking these pictures, however, should be apprised of your wishes. In order to best secure the pictures you desire, you should prepare a chronological list and present it in advance to the person taking your wedding pictures.

Also, the photographer should obey the "Code of Ethics for Wedding Photographers," which is as follows:

1. Contact the clergyman to learn of the rules, customs, and regulations of the particular church, and strictly obey these rules.

2. Work in a dignified, unobtrusive manner while taking the wedding and reception pictures. Popping flashbulbs during a ceremony are an intrusion. Shoot with available light or not at all.

3. Don't litter the church with discarded trash of any kind.

Be sure to have plenty of pictures taken. They tell your story and will be viewed many times through the years as you look back on this once-in-a-lifetime event.

Invitations and Announcements

It is customary for the bride's parents to pay for the invitations as well as bear the responsibility for addressing and mailing them. They should be sent out about five to six weeks prior to the wedding; at the very latest, no guest should receive an invitation later than two weeks before.

It is appropriate for the groom and his family to name about half of the guests to both wedding and reception. Therefore, consultation between the bride's mother and the groom's mother is essential. Since the bride's parents will be bearing the expense, it is customary for the bride's mother to call the groom's mother and explain the limitations on her own guest list and ask for one of approximate equal size. This list should provide complete addresses, including zip codes. The bride and her mother can then strike off any duplication of names.

Invitations should be mailed to anyone who may be expected to come to the wedding or reception.

Should the bride and her mother not be aware of the proper procedure for the mailing of invitations, it would be wise to either secure a book of etiquette from the library, consult with a bridal consultant or bridal shop, or talk with the people from whom you secure the invitations.

Attendants

The "bridal party" includes the bride, the groom, and their attendants, including ushers. In the simplest of weddings there should be at least two attendants, one for the bride and one for the groom. These usually sign the documents as witnesses. At more formal or ceremonial weddings, attendants can include as many of the following as desired:

16

Best Man
Groomsmen
Maid of Honor
Matron of Honor
Bridesmaids
Ushers
Candle Lighters
Flower Girl
Ring Bearer
Junior Bridesmaids
Junior Ushers
Page Boys (Trainbearers)

Rehearsal

The rehearsal is an important part of the planning for a successful wedding, particularly if it is to be an elaborate or even semiformal ceremony. If it is an informal wedding, a rehearsal would not be required, since the clergyman could give all necessary instructions in a short briefing before the ceremony.

At the rehearsal, all participants should be present so they can be apprised of their positions and the procedure for entering and leaving the sanctuary. This naturally includes the organist and soloist.

The words of the marriage service should not be used during the rehearsal, but the minister will explain each part in detail in order to avoid any confusion.

Wedding attire is not worn during the rehearsal; however, persons attending should be dressed nicely, not in blue jeans style.

The rehearsal usually is held in the evening and probably the night before the ceremony and, like all other items, must be cleared with the minister in advance.

The bride need not have a stand-in substitute for her.

It is well if the groom at this time would deliver to

the clergyman the marriage license and any other necessary legal papers that must be signed. It will help to avoid a slipup on the day of the wedding.

This would also be an excellent time for the bride's father to deliver checks to the organist, soloist, and any other persons that will be given a fee.

Paying the Bills

Listed here are the usual expenses that would be incurred by both the bride's family and the groom.

1. *The bride's family pays for:*

   Wedding invitations and announcements
   Bridal gown and trousseau
   All church expenses except the minister's fee
   Reception
   Wedding photographs
   Transportation to church (for bride and her attendants)
   Bride's gifts to the bridesmaids and maid of honor
   Floral decorations for the church and reception
   Gift for the groom
   Any other miscellaneous expenses not covered by the list for the groom.

2. *The groom pays for:*

   The bachelor dinner
   The clergyman's fee
   Flowers for:

   > Bride to wear on wedding trip
   > Both mothers and grandmothers
   > Boutonnieres for the best man, ushers, his father, and himself

   The wedding rings
   The honeymoon

Lodging for the best man and ushers if they live out
of town
The marriage license
A wedding present for the bride
Gifts for the best man and ushers.

Thank-you Notes

The thank-you note is an expression of appreciation
that should not be forgotten. Many people have been
asked to participate in your wedding, and they have given
of their time to help you have a successful wedding and
therefore should be promptly remembered.

These notes should be handwritten and express
specifically what you are thanking them for. Established
protocol requires that all thank-you notes be mailed within three weeks of your wedding.

It is the responsibility of the bride to acknowledge all
gifts, regardless by whom they were sent, including the
groom's family and relatives or friends.

You should mail thank-you notes as gifts are received;
and the notes for people in your wedding party should
either be handed to them immediately or mailed right
after the wedding.

Should you be in doubt as to who should receive a
thank-you note, it is best to go ahead and send one any-
way. It will create goodwill and may help to establish
lasting friendships. The *thank-you* is as important as anything else. Do not forget it.

2

The Ceremony

Standard ceremonies in Protestant churches follow a somewhat universal pattern. Using these as a starting point, adaptations and alterations can be made to fit the size and uniqueness of wedding desired. The details given below are presented as a general guide, inasmuch as there are many possible variations depending on the size, place, and formality of the wedding.

Assembling at the Church

The ushers should be instructed to arrive about an hour before the ceremony, attach their boutonnieres, and wait in the foyer, ready to seat the guests as they arrive.

The minister, groom, and best man should arrive at least 20 minutes before the wedding and wait in a room off of the altar end of the church. If a separate room is not available, they may wait in the minister's study.

The bride's attendants may assemble at the home of the bride or at the church. They may dress at either place along with the bride. The attendants should be instructed in advance.

If they meet at the home of the bride, then the bride, her parents, and the attendants leave the house at the same time. The bride's mother will leave in the first car, either alone or with one or two of the attendants. Following her will be the bride's attendants in other cars. The bride will be last, escorted by her father or whoever will give her away.

The bride's mother and the attendants should arrive about 10 minutes prior to the ceremony and assemble in a room off of the vestibule. The bride and her father arrive shortly and join them. If they dress at the church, the wedding party should be at the church one hour before the ceremony.

The groom's parents arrive before the bride. Upon arrival, they wait in the vestibule.

An usher should notify the groom and minister when the bride arrives.

Just before the time of the ceremony, the ushers close the doors to the sanctuary and seat no one else. Guests arriving last must seat themselves at the rear of the church.

One usher escorts the parents of the groom to their pew on the right side of the sanctuary.

Another usher then escorts the mother of the bride to her pew on the left.

Two ushers then march up the aisle side by side and unroll the aisle canvas from front to back.

The ushers may then join the bride's party, which should be lined up in the proper order as instructed at the rehearsal. Remember, if they are part of the aisle processional, ushers are never paired with bridesmaids. Pairing of ushers and attendants should be by height with the smallest taking the lead. Sometimes the ushers enter at the front with the groom and best man.

If candles are to be lighted, it should be determined by the bride with the consent of the minister as to the appropriate time. This is usually done immediately following the seating of the bride's mother.

The Processional

There are many possible variations of the following suggested procedure, and all of them may be correct. Positions taken by the ushers and bridesmaids at the altar depend upon the desires of the couple and the minister. The size and shape of the church must also be considered as well as the aisle arrangement (center or double aisle).

At the appointed hour, the organist lets the music fade and then begins the wedding march. Some brides prefer a soloist to sing an appropriate selection prior to the wedding march, and this is correct if desired.

As the organist begins the wedding march, the minister enters at right front, followed by the groom, who in turn is followed by the best man.

The minister takes his place on the platform (or chancel) or at the altar below (depending on where the vows will be taken), facing the congregation.

The groom stands on the minister's left (right of the aisle), angled toward the procession. The best man stands on the groom's left, one step farther from center, and one step nearer the pews.

The "hesitation" gait is outmoded today; however, the slow pace must be practiced if there is to be dignity to the processional. Spacing of the procession must be determined by the size and style of the church. The minister can instruct you at this point.

The usual order of the procession is:

1. Ushers (if part of the processional) are paired and take positions to the right of the best man, facing the remaining procession.

2. The bridesmaids may be paired, or enter singly, depending on the number, taking positions on the left side. (If the ushers divide, then the bridesmaids divide also and stand in front of the ushers.)

22

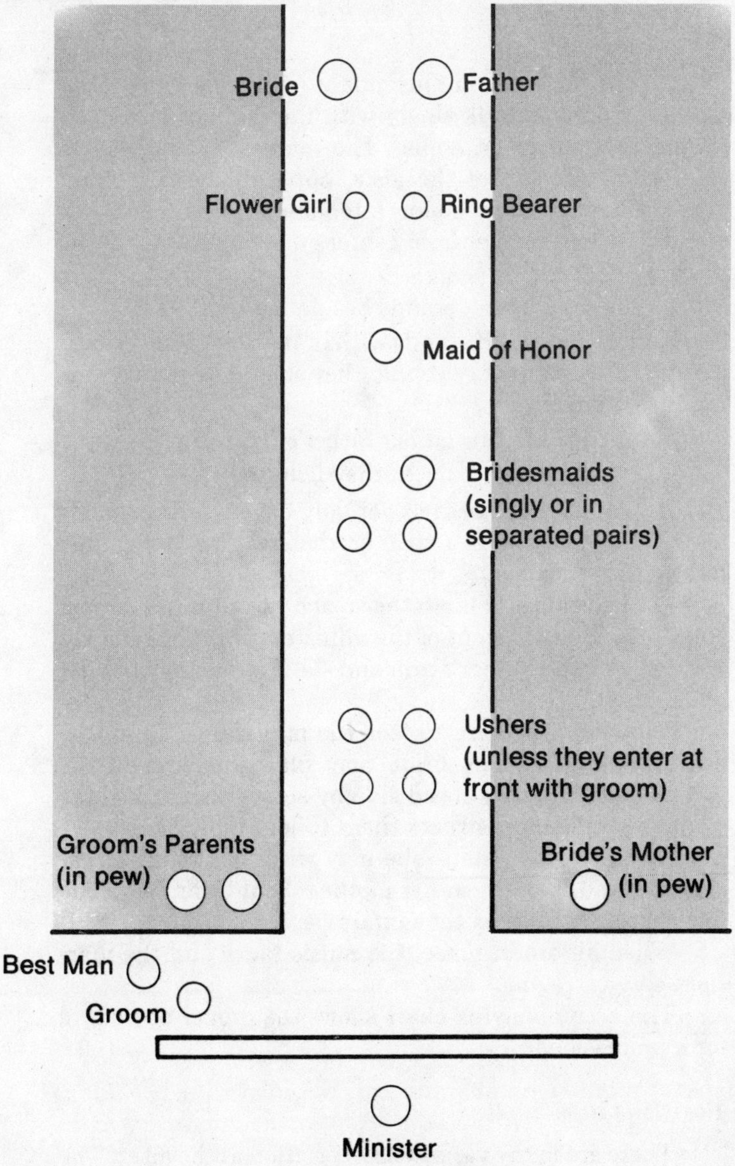

Bridal Procession

3. The bride's honor attendant (if there are two, they may be paired or walk singly with the maid of honor following the matron of honor. The maid of honor takes a position to the left of the aisle, opposite the best man. When there are two honor attendants, the second one stands one step farther from center and one step nearer the pews.

4. The ring bearer stands beside the best man.

5. The flower girl stands with or in front of the bridesmaids. (If they are very young, they should be seated during the ceremony.)

6. The bride leans on her father's right arm.

7. If page boys are used, they hold the train.

If a ring bearer does not actually have the rings and is very young, he takes a seat at the front as designated during the rehearsal.

As the bride and her father reach the altar, the groom steps toward her in front of the minister. She then removes her arm from her father's arm and shifts her bouquet to her left side.

Together they turn to face the minister as do all the other attendants. The bride may place her arm in the groom's, or they may stand side by side without touching until the minister instructs them to join right hands.

(As the bride enters, she may wish for the congregation to stand. If so, then her mother should stand as a cue to the congregation as the fanfare begins.)

When all are in place, the music fades and the marriage service begins.

The accompanying chart shows the proper procedure for a processional.

Positions at the Altar

There are many variations in position at the altar. The

wishes of the clergyman who shall officiate should be honored. The standard formation is shown in the chart.

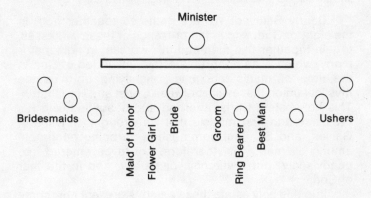

Positions at the Altar During Ceremony

Marriage Service

The main parts of the marriage ceremony are the minister's preamble, the charge, the exchange of vows, the marriage pronouncement, and the blessings.

There is a contemporary trend for couples to write some of their own marriage ceremony, particularly their personal vows. While many ministers will cooperate in part or whole, it is necessary first that the minister approve a ceremony other than the traditional or standard one. The standard sequence will, in any case, be followed. Even if the traditional wording is used, there are many things that can be added to heighten the beauty of the ceremony.

Here is the standard ceremony as printed in the church *Manual.* It is beautiful and thoroughly adequate as it is, but may be modified if desired.

At the day and time appointed for the solemnization of matrimony, the persons to be married—having been qualified according to law —standing together, the man on the right hand and the woman on the left, the minister shall address the congregation as follows:

Dearly Beloved: We are gathered together here in the sight of God, and in the presence of these witnesses, to join together this man and this woman, in holy matrimony, which is an honorable estate, instituted of God in the time of man's innocency, signifying unto us the mystical union that exists between Christ and His Church. This holy estate Christ adorned and beautified with His presence and first miracle that He wrought, in Cana of Galilee, and St. Paul commended as being honorable among all men. It is, therefore, not to be entered into unadvisedly, but reverently, discreetly, and in the fear of God.

Into this holy estate these persons present now come to be joined.

Addressing the couple to be married, the minister shall say:

——— and ———, I require and charge you both that, if either of you knows any impediment why you may not be lawfully joined together in matrimony, you do now confess it; for be well assured that so many as are coupled together otherwise than God's Word allows are not joined together by God, neither is their matrimony lawful.

If no impediment be alleged, then shall the minister say unto the man:

———, will you have this woman to be your wedded wife, to live together after God's ordinance in the holy estate of matrimony? Will you love her, comfort her, honor and keep her, in sickness and in health; and, forsaking all others, keep yourself only unto her, so long as you both shall live?
Response: I will.

Then shall the minister say unto the woman:

———, will you have this man to be your wedded husband, to live together after God's ordinance in the holy estate of matrimony? Will you love, honor, and keep him, in sickness and in health; and, forsaking all others, keep yourself only unto him, so long as you both shall live?

Response: I will.

Then shall the minister ask:

Who gives this woman to be married to this man?

Response (by the father, or whoever gives the bride in marriage): I do.

Facing each other and joining right hands, the couple shall then exchange the following vows:

The man shall repeat after the minister:

I, ———, take you, ———, to be my wedded wife, to have and to hold from this day forward, for better—for worse, for richer—for poorer, in sickness and in health, to love and to cherish, till death us do part, according to God's holy ordinance; and thereto I pledge you my faith.

The woman shall repeat after the minister:

I, ———, take you, ———, to be my wedded husband, to have and to hold from this day forward, for better—for worse, for richer—for poorer, in sickness and in health, to love and to cherish, till death us do part, according to God's holy ordinance; and thereto I pledge you my faith.

If desired, a ring ceremony may be inserted at this point. The minister receives the ring from the groomsman and, in turn, passes it to the groom. As he then places it upon the bride's finger, he shall repeat after the minister:

This ring I give you as a token of my love and as a pledge of my constant fidelity.

The couple then shall kneel as the minister offers the following, or an extemporaneous prayer:

O Eternal God, Creator, and Preserver of all mankind, Giver of all spiritual grace, the Author of everlasting life, send Thy blessing upon these Thy servants, this man and this woman, whom we now bless in Thy name; that, as Isaac and Rebekah lived faithfully together, so these persons may surely perform and keep the vow and covenant made between them this hour and may ever remain in love and peace together, through Jesus Christ our Lord. Amen.

Then shall the minister say:

Forasmuch as this man and woman have consented together in holy wedlock, and have witnessed the same before God and this company, and have declared the same by joining of hands, I pronounce that they are husband and wife together, in the name of the Father, and of the Son, and of the Holy Spirit. Those whom God has joined together let not man put asunder. Amen.

The minister shall then add his blessing:

God, the Father, the Son, and the Holy Spirit, bless, preserve, and keep you; the Lord mercifully with His favor look upon you, and fill you with all spiritual benediction and grace. May you so live together in this life that in the world to come you may have life everlasting.

The minister may then conclude with an extemporaneous prayer and/or benediction.

If the couple wishes to, they may kneel during this benediction, or they may remain standing. After this the minister will usually say, "You may now kiss the bride." The kiss is not to be a long one. If the bride wears a veil, it is proper for her to turn to her maid of honor and receive help from her in raising the veil before the kiss. After the kiss, the clergyman will usually introduce the couple to the congregation.

It is also proper for the minister to extend his congratulations and best wishes prior to the recessional if he wishes to do so.

Groom ○ ○ Bride

Ring Bearer ○ ○ Flower Girl

Best Man ○ ○ Maid of Honor

○ ○

Ushers ○ ○ Bridesmaids

○ ○

○ ○

(Minister may remain until parents are
ushered out, then go to vestry.)

The Recessional

Recessional

After the introduction by the minister, the bride will retrieve her bouquet from the maid of honor. It is customary for the maid of honor to lift the bride's train out of her way as she turns to make her way down the aisle. The bride will take the groom's right arm.

As the organist begins the recessional music, the bride and groom start the exit march. They should not move swiftly, but at a faster pace than in the processional. (If desired, they may briefly stop to receive congratulations from her parents and then his.)

The accompanying diagram shows the order of the recessional.

Unless there is a receiving line, or pictures to be taken following the wedding ceremony, the bride and groom and her attendants go immediately to the waiting cars and go to the place where the reception will be held, leaving only those ushers who have been assigned special duties.

Following the wedding party's exit, one usher will come back up the aisle and escort the bride's mother out on his right arm, with her father following a pace behind. Another usher then comes to escort the groom's mother out, with the groom's father following a pace behind. It is in good taste to also escort the grandmothers in the same fashion. The ushers may then release the audience a row at a time, or there may be a general dismissal.

Receiving Line

A receiving line at the church is optional. Usually if there is a reception to follow the ceremony, a receiving line is set up there rather than at the church. The proper order of this line is as indicated in the following charts.

Bride's Mother Bride's Father Groom's Mother Groom's Father Bride Groom Maid of Honor Bridesmaids

◯◯◯ ◯ ◯ ◯ ◯   ◯ ◯ ◯ ◯

Flow →

Receiving Line

The father of the bride may or may not stand in line according to his personal wishes. Bride should always be on groom's right. Best man, ushers, and children do not stand in the line.

3

A Countdown Checklist

The following list of "things to be done" includes most of the major steps in wedding preparation and is given in time sequence. Each wedding is different, and so you may have to adapt and perhaps expand or cut this list to suit your own needs. It is important to work with a plan so that items can be checked off as they are taken care of.

Three to six months prior to the wedding:

1. Determine the type and size of wedding and reception that is suited to your tastes. Be realistic when figuring the expenses, for costs are steadily rising and will probably be higher than you anticipate.

2. The bride and groom should choose the wedding date, keeping in mind that it must first be cleared with the minister.

3. Check with the minister to make sure that both he and the church will be available on the date you have selected. Should you find that date taken, you will naturally have to alter your plans. Bear in mind that the minister is a busy person and may already have the date you have selected scheduled.

4. The bride and groom should make an appointment to see the minister together for personal counseling

and discussion of wedding details. At this session you should clear the date for the rehearsal and check on various fees and services available.

5. Make reservations for the use of the building you will hold your reception in, if in a place other than the church fellowship hall. Check on the service available and costs that will be incurred.

6. Check with the florist and make a reservation for flowers, decorations, and any other services you may desire.

7. Select a photographer and reserve the time and date for the wedding.

8. Once the day and time of the wedding has been confirmed with the minister, the bride can issue formal invitations to her attendants. The groom should also issue invitations to his best man and ushers.

9. A guest list should be compiled by the bride, groom, and both families. The bride's mother should set a date for the groom and his parents to complete their guest list.

10. Order invitations, announcements (if used), and thank-you notes.

11. Begin looking for a house or apartment, and the style of furniture you will be interested in.

12. If you are buying your wedding dress and bridesmaids' dresses, now is the time to begin shopping for them. If they are being made, you should begin immediately. Your wedding dress should be finished at least six weeks before the wedding if you are sending a portrait to the local newspapers. This will allow time for the photographer to develop the formal pose.

13. The bride's mother should select her dress and inform the mother of the groom its color, style, and length.

14. The bride, with her mother, should begin to

address invitations so they will be ready for mailing. Do not mail them yet.

Two months prior to the wedding:

15. Order the gifts you will present to the brides-maids. If you will be giving a gift to the groom, it should be ordered at this time also.

16. The groom should order the wedding present for his bride and gifts for the best man and the ushers.

17. The groom should order the bride's bouquet.

18. The bride's parents should order the flowers to be worn at the wedding.

19. Wedding rings should be selected and ordered if this matter has not already been handled. You should allow two to three weeks for engraving and delivery.

20. Complete the purchase or schedule fittings for the bridesmaids' dresses if they are being made.

21. The groom decides on a firm where the formal clothes for himself, his best man, and ushers are to be rented. He should notify these gentlemen as to when they will be fitted. He should also choose the style and color.

22. If blood tests are necessary (and in most states they are required), make an appointment with the doctor.

23. Schedule an appointment with the hairdresser for the day preceding the wedding.

24. If you are planning a honeymoon, the groom should make reservations where required.

25. The bride and groom make final arrangements for securing a house or apartment. Order your furniture to be delivered in advance.

26. A new will should be drafted by a competent lawyer.

27. Take care of matters pertaining to insurance.

Instruct the agent to make the effective date, the day of the wedding. Don't forget hospitalization insurance.

28. Mail the invitations about five weeks prior to the wedding.

The last four to six weeks prior to the wedding:

29. If you have had a formal wedding portrait made, send it to the newspaper. You may take it in person if you wish. Be sure to give the newspaper all pertinent details.

30. Make arrangements for housing of out-of-town attendants, best man, and the ushers.

31. Secure a gift record book. Be sure to keep it up to date. Select a young lady to care for the guest book at the wedding.

32. Write thank-you notes each day that gifts arrive.

33. If you are planning a rehearsal dinner or breakfast, reservations should be made by the groom's parents if they are to give it. Otherwise, the bride's parents should make the arrangements.

34. Check with the manager of the place where the reception is to be held about various details such as seating arrangements, placement of the wedding cake, food (if it is to be served), the place to set up the receiving line (if one was not used at the church), the parking of cars, etc.

35. Give the florist final instructions as to the time and place of delivery for flowers and any other items you have ordered.

36. Give the organist and soloist instructions concerning special numbers to be used during the ceremony. Apprise them of when they will be playing or singing, as the case may be. This matter will have already been cleared with the minister.

37. Make the final arrangements with the bridesmaids as to where they will dress and where they will

receive their bouquets. Clear the matter of transportation to the ceremony and give each of them a detailed list of instructions.

38. The groom gives similar instructions to the ushers.

39. Keep the appointment for the blood tests or any other medical reports that might be necessary.

40. Prepare a list of guests who should receive special attention or who should be seated in a special place. Give this list to the ushers.

41. The bride and groom goes together to the city hall or county courthouse to get the marriage license about a week before the wedding. Naturally this is determined by local regulations.

The week before the wedding:

42. The bride should change her name on all credit cards, magazine subscriptions, charge accounts, insurance policies (to become effective on the date of the wedding), social security card, etc. Also, remember to change your driver's license after the honeymoon.

43. Check with all suppliers—florist, place of reception, organist, soloist, and photographer—to be sure that all arrangements are understood.

44. Make out the place cards, if any, for the reception.

45. The groom makes a final check with the firm supplying the clothing of the groom, best man, and ushers.

46. Prepare a list of items you will take on your wedding trip.

47. Assemble the items you may need for the wedding rehearsal.

48. Prepare envelopes with fees for the janitor or custodian, organist, soloist, and any other people on the church staff whose services you have requested.

49. The groom prepares the envelope with the fee for the minister.

50. Review this entire list to make sure you have not forgotten anything.

Have a beautiful wedding!